P.14   P.30

FAVOURITE HYMNS

THIS PUBLICATION IS NOT AUTHORISED FOR
SALE IN THE UNITED STATES OF AMERICA AND/OR CANADA

HAL LEONARD EUROPE
Distributed by Music Sales

ABIDE WITH ME

Words by HENRY F. LYTE
Music by W.H. MONK

Copyright © 1983 by HAL LEONARD CORPORATION
International Copyright Secured   All Rights Reserved

ALL CREATURES
OF OUR GOD AND KING

Words by FRANCIS OF ASSISI
Music from *Geistliche Kirchengesäng*

Copyright © 1997 by HAL LEONARD CORPORATION
International Copyright Secured   All Rights Reserved

ALL THINGS BRIGHT AND BEAUTIFUL

Words by CECIL FRANCES ALEXANDER
17th Century English Melody
Arranged by MARTIN SHAW

Copyright © 1991 by HAL LEONARD CORPORATION
International Copyright Secured   All Rights Reserved

AMAZING GRACE

Words by JOHN NEWTON
Traditional American Melody

Copyright © 1991 by HAL LEONARD CORPORATION
International Copyright Secured All Rights Reserved

Verse 3
And when this flesh and heart shall fail
and mortal life shall cease.
I shall possess within the veil
a life of joy and peace.

When we've been there ten thousand years,
bright shining as the sun.

We've no less days to sing God's praise
than when we first begun.

BATTLE HYMN OF THE REPUBLIC

Words by JULIA WARD HOWE
Music by WILLIAM STEFFE

1. Mine eyes have seen the glo - ry of the com - ing of the Lord. He is
2. seen him in the watch-fires of the hun - dred cir - cling camps. They have
3.-5. *(See additional lyrics)*

tramp - ling out the vin - tage where the grapes of wrath are stored. He hath
build - ed Him an al - tar in the eve - ning dews and damps. I have

loos'd the fate - ful light - ning of His ter - ri - ble swift sword. His
read His right - eous sen - tence by the dim and flar - ing lamps. His

Copyright © 1995 by HAL LEONARD CORPORATION
International Copyright Secured   All Rights Reserved

Additional Lyrics

3. I have read a fiery gospel writ in burnished rows of steel.
   As ye deal with my contempters, so with you my grace shall deal.
   Let the hero born of woman crush the serpent with his heel,
   Since God is marching on.

4. He has sounded forth the trumpet that shall never call retreat
   He is sifting out the hearts of men before His judgement seat.
   O be swift, my soul, to answer Him, be jubilant, my feet.
   Our God is marching on.

5. In the beauty of the lilies, Christ was born across the sea.
   With a glory in His bosom that transfigures you and me.
   As He died to make men holy, let us die to make men free,
   While God is marching on.

BE THOU MY VISION

Traditional Irish

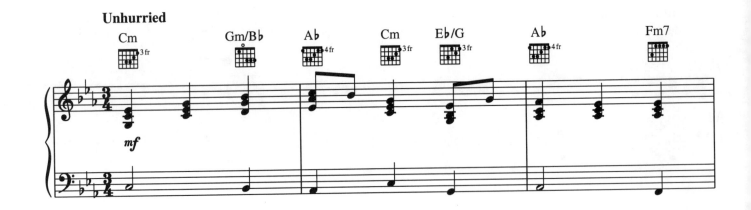

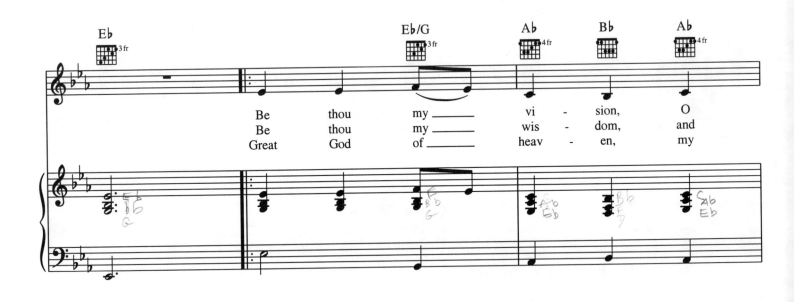

Be thou my _____ vi - sion, O
Be thou my _____ wis - dom, and
Great God of _____ heav - en, my

Lord of my heart; naught be all else to me,
thou my true word; I ev - er with thee and
vic - to - ry won, may I reach heav - en's joys,

Copyright © 1997 by HAL LEONARD CORPORATION
International Copyright Secured All Rights Reserved

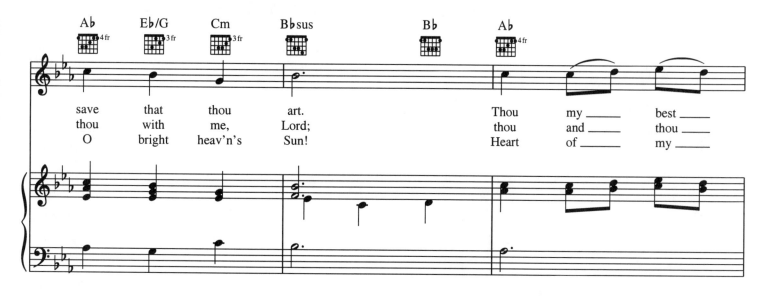

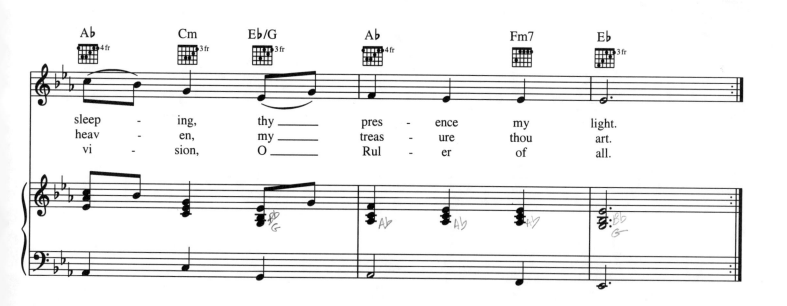

CHRIST THE LORD IS RISEN TODAY

Words by CHARLES WESLEY
Music adapted from *Lyra Davidica*

Copyright © 1983 by HAL LEONARD CORPORATION
International Copyright Secured   All Rights Reserved

2. Lives again our glorious King: Alleluia!
   Where, O death, is now thy sting? Alleluia!
   Dying once, He all doth save: Alleluia!
   Where thy victory, O grave? Alleluia!

3. Love's redeeming work is done, Alleluia!
   Fought the fight, the battle won: Alleluia!
   Death in vain forbids Him rise: Alleluia!
   Christ has opened Paradise. Alleluia!

4. Soar we now, where Christ has led, Alleluia!
   Foll'wing our exalted Head: Alleluia!
   Made like Him, like Him we rise: Alleluia!
   Ours the cross, the grave, the skies. Alleluia!

THE CHURCH'S ONE FOUNDATION

Words by SAMUEL STONE
Music by SAMUEL WESLEY

Copyright © 1986 by HAL LEONARD CORPORATION
International Copyright Secured All Rights Reserved

2. Elect from every nation,
   Yet one o'er all the earth,
   Her charter of salvation,
   One Lord, one faith, one birth;
   One holy name she blesses,
   Partakes one holy food,
   And to one hope she presses,
   With every grace endued.

3. 'Mid toil and tribulation,
   And tumult of her war,
   She waits the consummation
   Of peace for evermore;
   Till with the vision glorious,
   Her longing eyes are blest,
   And the great Church victorious
   Shall be the Church at rest.

4. Yet she on earth hath union
   With God, the Three in One,
   And mystic sweet communion
   With those whose rest is won;
   O happy ones and holy!
   Lord give us grace that we
   Like them, the meek and lowly,
   On high may dwell with Thee.

CROWN HIM WITH MANY CROWNS

Words by MATTHEW BRIDGES and GODFREY THRING
Music by GEORGE JOB ELVEY

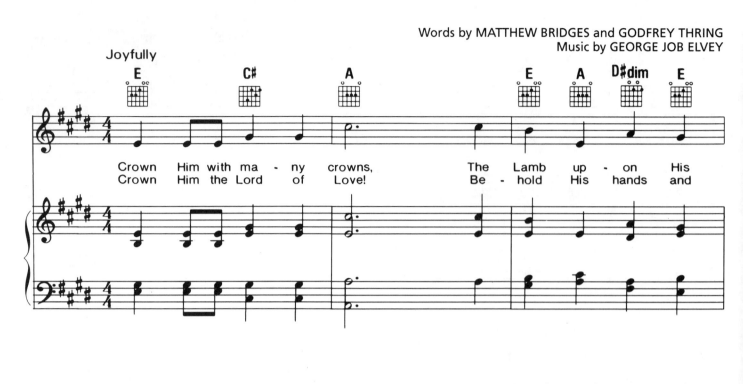

Crown Him with ma - ny crowns, The Lamb up - on His
Crown Him the Lord of Love! Be - hold His hands and

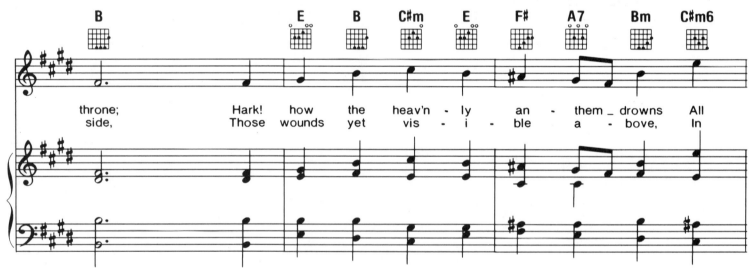

throne; Hark! how the heav'n - ly an - them _ drowns, All
side, Those wounds yet vis - i - ble a - bove, In

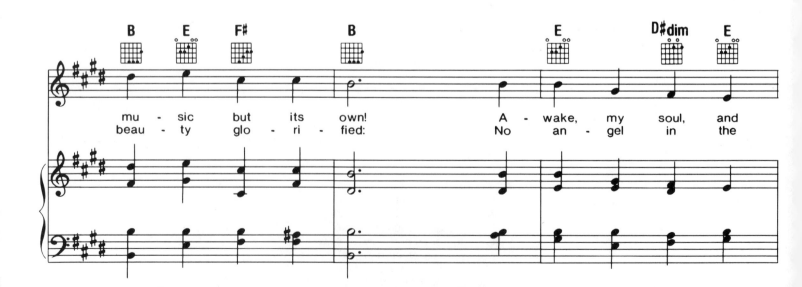

mu - sic but its own! A - wake, my soul, and
beau - ty glo - ri - fied: No an - gel in the

Copyright © 1983 by HAL LEONARD CORPORATION
International Copyright Secured   All Rights Reserved

3. Crown Him the Lord of life, Who triumphed o'er the grave
   And rose victorious in the strife for those He came to save.
   His glories now we sing, Who dies and rose on high,
   Who dies eternal life to bring and lives that death may die.

HOLY, HOLY, HOLY

Text by REGINALD HEBER
Music by JOHN B. DYKES

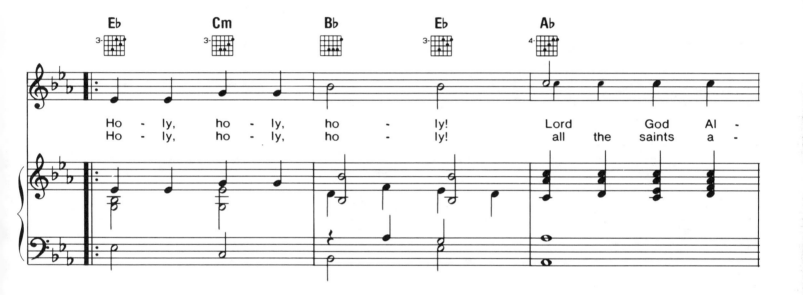

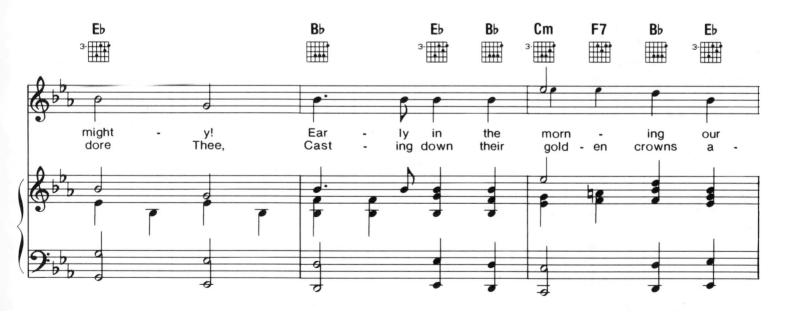

Copyright © 1983 by HAL LEONARD CORPORATION
International Copyright Secured   All Rights Reserved

ETERNAL FATHER, STRONG TO SAVE

Words by W. WHITING
Music by J.B. DYKES

Copyright © 1996 by HAL LEONARD CORPORATION
International Copyright Secured   All Rights Reserved

Additional Verses

2. O Savior, whose almighty word
   The winds and waves submissive heard,
   Who walkedst on the foaming deep
   And calm amid its rage didst sleep:
   O hear us when we cry to Thee
   For those in peril on the sea.

3. O sacred Spirit, who didst brood
   Upon the chaos dark and rude,
   Who bad'st its angry tumult cease,
   And gavest light and life and peace:
   O hear us when we cry to Thee
   For those in peril on the sea.

4. O Trinity of love and power,
   Our brethren shield in danger's hour;
   From rock and tempest, fire and foe,
   Protect them wheresoe'er they go;
   And ever let there rise to Thee
   Glad hymns of praise from land and sea. Amen.

FAIREST LORD JESUS

Words from *Münster Gesangbuch* (v. 1-3)
Words for v. 4 by JOSEPH AUGUST SEISS
Music from *Schlesische Volkslieder*

Warmly

Fair — est Lord Je — sus, Ru — ler of all
Fair are the mead — ows, Fair — er still the
Fair is the sun — shine, Fair — er still the
Beau — ti — ful Sav — ior! Lord _____ of the

na — ture, O Thou of God and _____
wood — lands, Robed in the bloom — ing _____
moon — light, And all the twin — kling _____
na — tions! Son of _____ God and _____

Copyright © 1999 by HAL LEONARD CORPORATION
International Copyright Secured   All Rights Reserved

FOR THE BEAUTY OF THE EARTH

Text by FOLLIOT S. PIERPOINT
Music by CONRAD KOCHER

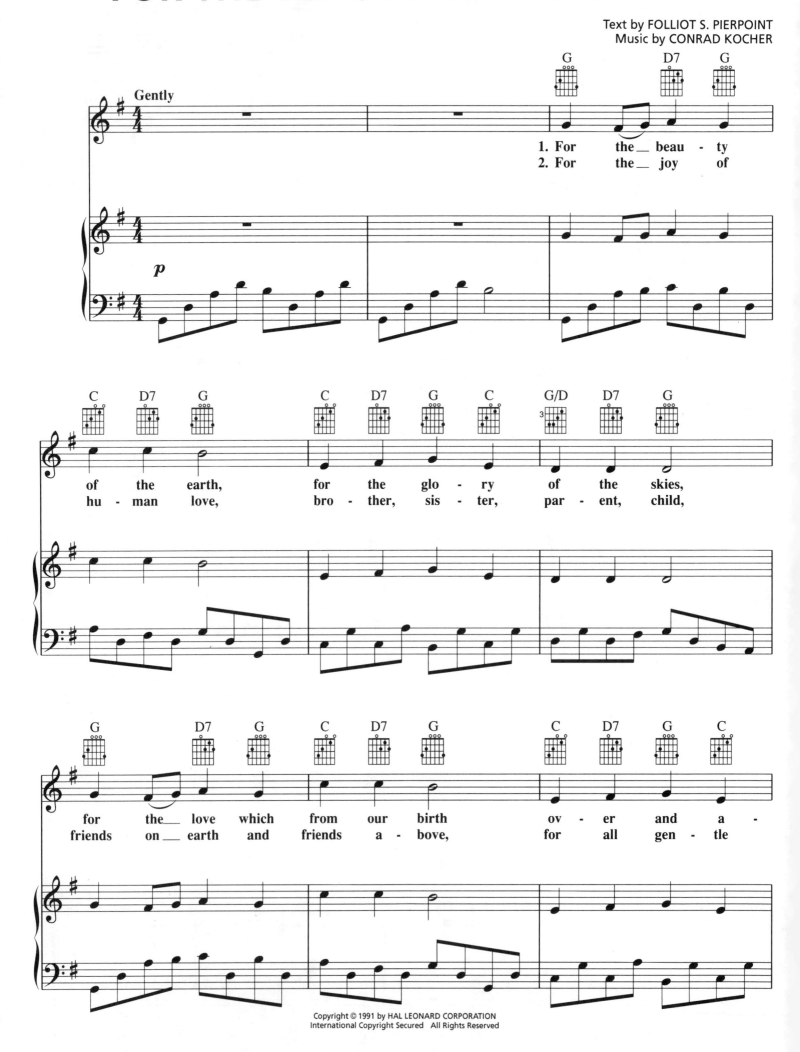

Copyright © 1991 by HAL LEONARD CORPORATION
International Copyright Secured All Rights Reserved

GUIDE ME, O THOU GREAT JEHOVAH

Words by WILLIAM WILLIAMS
Music by JOHN HUGHES

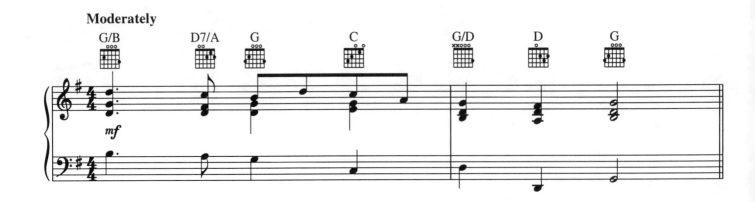

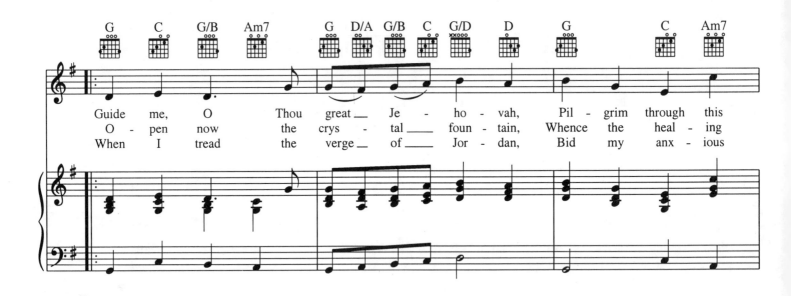

Guide me, O Thou great ___ Je - ho - vah, Pil - grim through this
O - pen now the crys - tal ___ foun - tain, Whence the heal - ing
When I tread the verge ___ of ___ Jor - dan, Bid my anx - ious

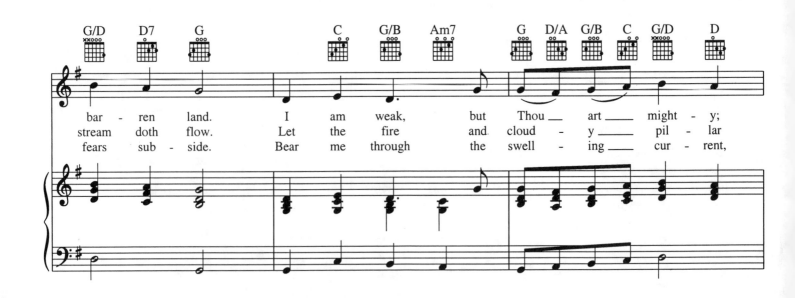

bar - ren land. I am weak, but Thou ___ art ___ might - y;
stream doth flow. Let the fire and cloud - y ___ pil - lar
fears sub - side. Bear me through the swell - ing ___ cur - rent,

Copyright © 1999 by HAL LEONARD CORPORATION
International Copyright Secured   All Rights Reserved

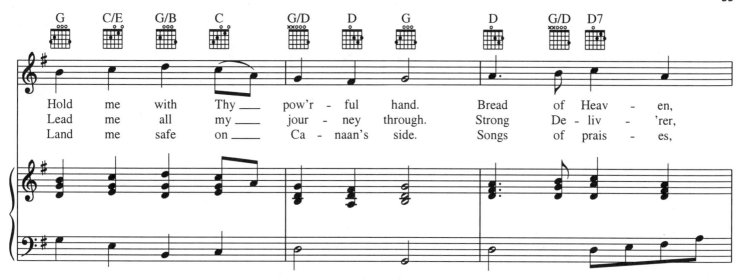

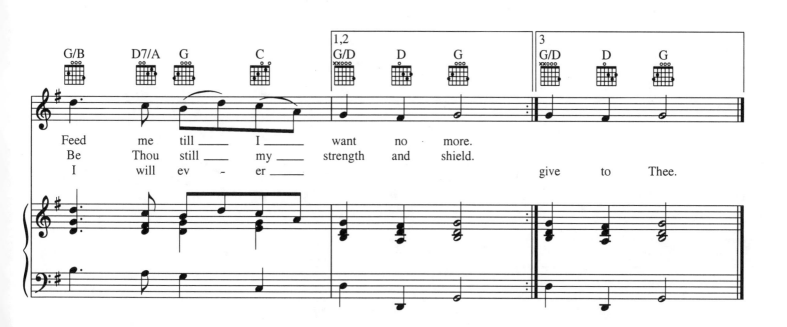

HOW SWEET THE NAME
OF JESUS SOUNDS

Words by JOHN NEWTON
Music by ALEXANDER REINAGLE

Copyright © 1983 by HAL LEONARD CORPORATION
International Copyright Secured   All Rights Reserved

IMMORTAL, INVISIBLE

Words by WALTER CHALMERS SMITH
Traditional Music

With strength

Im - mor - tal, in -
rest - ing, un -
all, life Thou
reign - est in

vis - i - ble, God on - ly wise, In
hast - ing, and si - lent as light, Nor
giv - est, to both great and small; In
glo - ry; Thou dwell - est in light; Thine

light in - ac - ces - si - ble hid from our
want - ing nor wast - ing, Thou rul - est in
all life Thou liv - est, the true life of
an - gels a - dore Thee, all veil - ing their

Copyright © 1997 by HAL LEONARD CORPORATION
International Copyright Secured All Rights Reserved

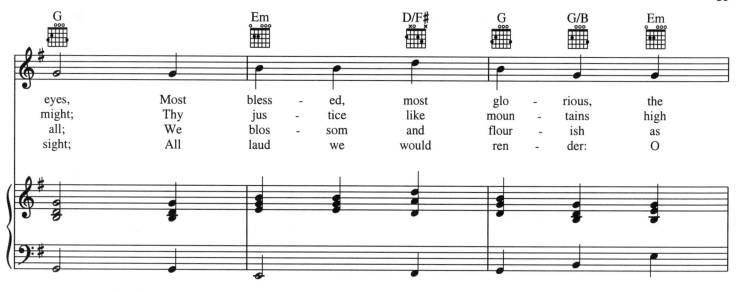

eyes, Most bless - ed, most glo - rious, the
might; Thy jus - tice like moun - tains high
all; We blos - som and flour - ish as
sight; All laud we would ren - der: O

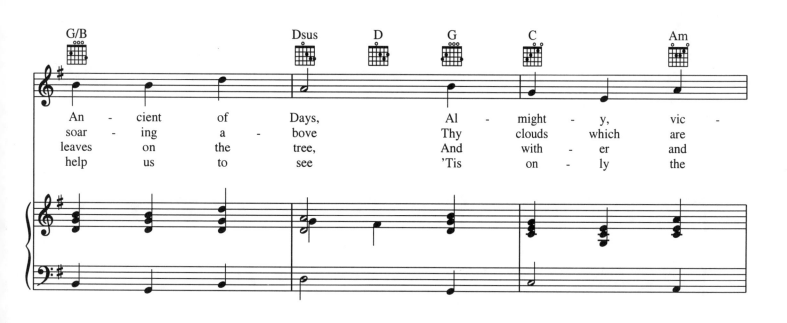

An - cient of Days, Al - might - y, vic -
soar - ing a - bove Thy clouds which are
leaves on the tree, And with - er and
help us to see 'Tis on - ly the

to - rious, Thy great Name we praise. Un -
foun - tains of good - ness and love. To
per - ish, but naught chang - eth Thee. To Thou
splen - dor of light hid - eth Thee.

JOYFUL, JOYFUL, WE ADORE THEE

Words by HENRY VAN DYKE
Music by LUDWIG VAN BEETHOVEN,
melody from Ninth Symphony
Adapted by EDWARD HODGES

Copyright © 1999 by HAL LEONARD CORPORATION
International Copyright Secured   All Rights Reserved

THE LORD'S MY SHEPHERD, I'LL NOT WANT

Text based on *Scottish Psalter,* 1650
Music by JESSIE S. IRVINE

Copyright © 1999 by HAL LEONARD CORPORATION
International Copyright Secured   All Rights Reserved

LOVE DIVINE, ALL LOVES EXCELLING

Words by CHARLES WESLEY
Music by JOHN ZUNDEL

Copyright © 1999 by HAL LEONARD CORPORATION
International Copyright Secured   All Rights Reserved

A MIGHTY FORTRESS IS OUR GOD

Words and Music by
MARTIN LUTHER

Copyright © 1983 by HAL LEONARD CORPORATION
International Copyright Secured   All Rights Reserved

3. And tho this world, with devils filled,
Should threaten to undo us;
We will not fear, for God hath willed
His truth to triumph through us;
The Prince of darkness grim,
We tremble not for him;
His rage we can endure,
For lo! His doom is sure,
One little word shall fell him.

4. That word above all earthly powers,
No thanks to them abideth,
The spirit and the gifts are ours
Through Him who with us sideth;
Let goods and kindred go,
This mortal life also;
The body they may kill;
God's truth abideth still,
His kingdom is forever.

NEARER MY GOD TO THEE

Text by SARAH F. ADAMS
Music by LOWELL MASON

Copyright © 1983 by HAL LEONARD CORPORATION
International Copyright Secured   All Rights Reserved

49

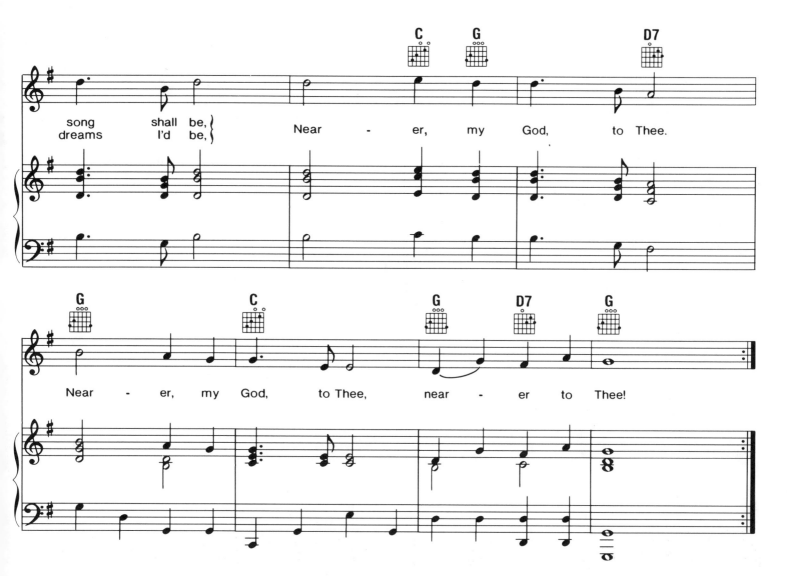

3. Then with my waking tho'ts
   Bright with Thy praise,
   Out of my stony griefs
   Bethel I'll raise
   So by my woes to be,
   Nearer, my God, to Thee,
   Nearer, my God, to Thee,
   Nearer to Thee!

4. Or if on joyful wing,
   Cleaving the sky,
   Sun, moon, and stars forgot,
   Upwards I'll fly,
   Still all my song shall be,
   Nearer, my God, to Thee,
   Nearer, my God, to Thee,
   Nearer to Thee!

NOW THANK WE ALL OUR GOD

German Words by MARTIN RINKART
English Translation by CATHERINE WINKWORTH
Music by JOHANN CRÜGER

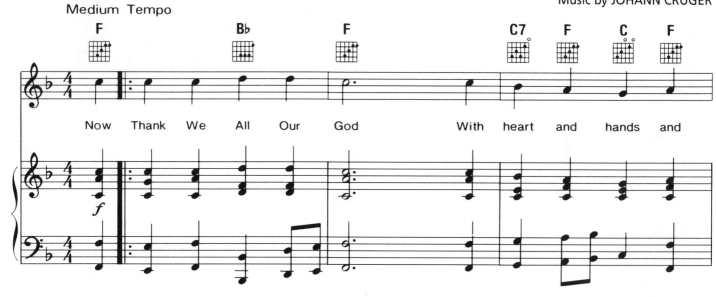

Copyright © 1983 by HAL LEONARD CORPORATION
International Copyright Secured   All Rights Reserved

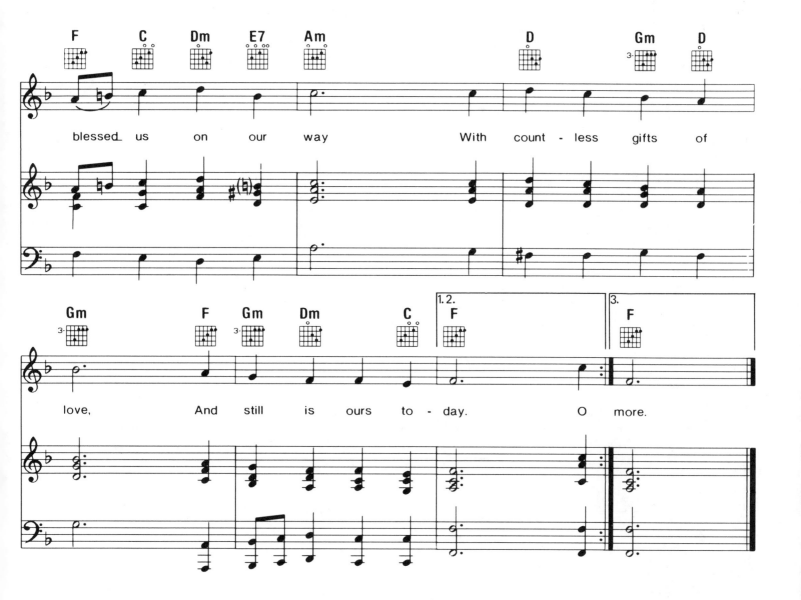

blessed us on our way With count-less gifts of

love, And still is ours to-day. O more.

2. (O) may this bounteous God
   Through all our life be near us,
   With ever joyful hearts
   And blessed peace to cheer us;
   And keep us in His grace,
   And guide us when perplexed,
   And free us from all ills,
   In this world and the next.

3. (All) praise and thanks to God
   The Father now be given,
   The Son and Him who reigns
   With them in highest heaven;
   The one eternal God,
   Whom earth and heav'n adore;
   For thus it was, is now,
   And shall be evermore.

O FOR A THOUSAND TONGUES TO SING

Text by CHARLES WESLEY
Music by CARL G. GLÄSER

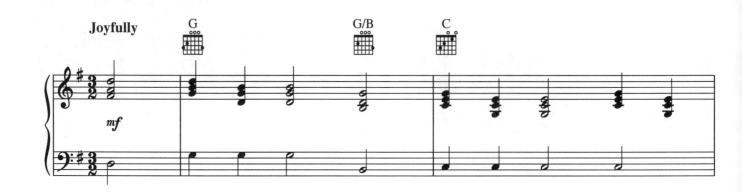

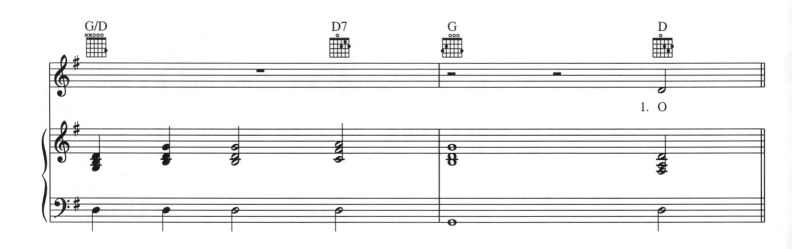

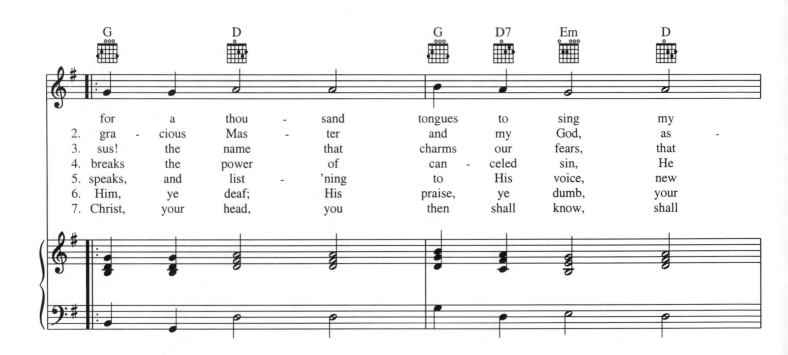

	for	a	thou-	sand	tongues	to	sing	my
2.	gra-	cious	Mas-	ter	and	my	God,	as-
3.	sus!	the	name	that	charms	our	fears,	that
4.	breaks	the	power	of	can-	celed	sin,	He
5.	speaks,	and	list-	'ning	to	His	voice,	new
6.	Him,	ye	deaf;	His	praise,	ye	dumb,	your
7.	Christ,	your	head,	you	then	shall	know,	shall

Copyright © 1997 by HAL LEONARD CORPORATION
International Copyright Secured   All Rights Reserved

O GOD, OUR HELP IN AGES PAST

Words by ISAAC WATTS
Melody attributed to WILLIAM CROFT

Copyright © 1991 by HAL LEONARD CORPORATION
International Copyright Secured   All Rights Reserved

O JESUS, I HAVE PROMISED

Words by JOHN E. BODE
Music by ARTHUR H. MANN

Copyright © 1999 by HAL LEONARD CORPORATION
International Copyright Secured   All Rights Reserved

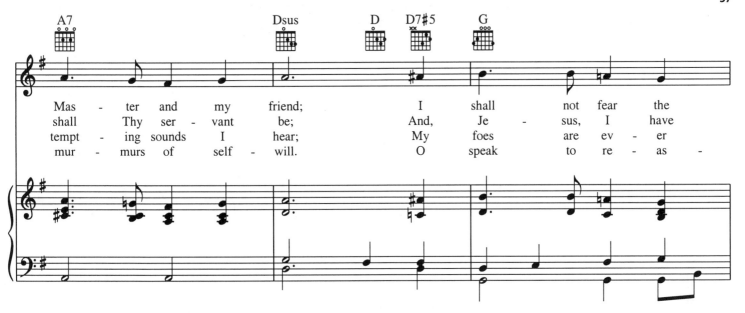

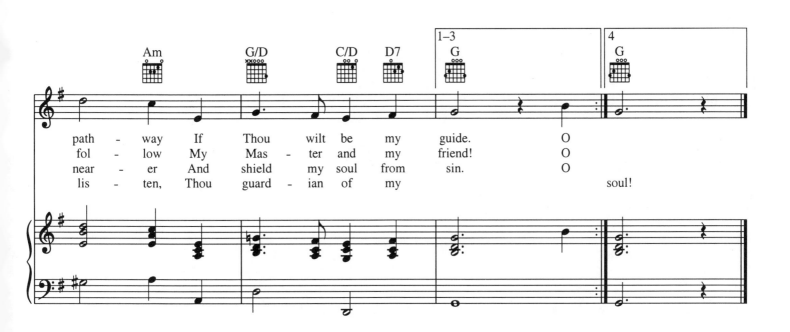

O SACRED HEAD, NOW WOUNDED

Words by BERNARD OF CLAIRVAUX
Music by HANS HASSLER

Copyright © 1991 by HAL LEONARD CORPORATION
International Copyright Secured   All Rights Reserved

O WORSHIP THE KING

Words by ROBERT GRANT
Based on "Lyons,"
Attributed to JOHANN MICHAEL HAYDN

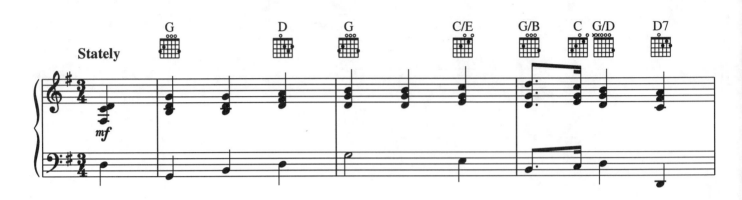

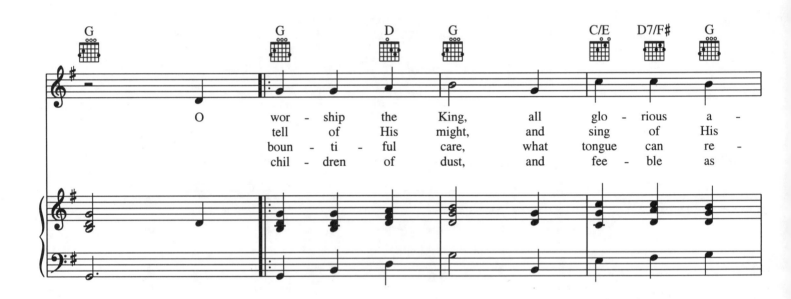

O wor - ship the King, all glo - rious a -
tell of His might, and sing of His
boun - ti - ful care, what tongue can re -
chil - dren of dust, and fee - ble as

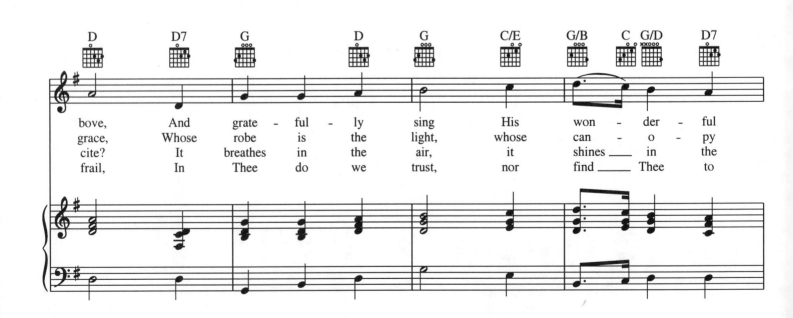

bove, And grate - ful - ly sing His won - der - ful
grace, Whose robe is the light, whose can - o - py
cite? It breathes in the air, whose it shines ___ in the
frail, In Thee do we trust, nor find ___ Thee to

Copyright © 1999 by HAL LEONARD CORPORATION
International Copyright Secured   All Rights Reserved

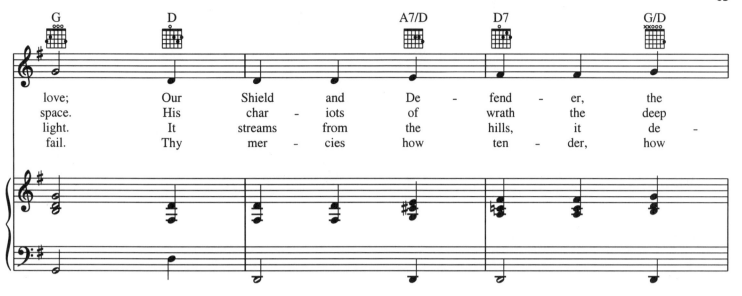

love; Our Shield and De - fend - er, the
space. His char - iots of wrath the deep
light. It streams from the hills, it de -
fail. Thy mer - cies how ten - der, how

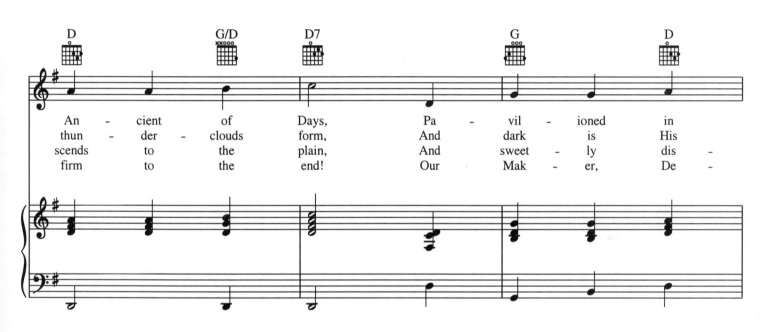

An - cient of Days, Pa - vil - ioned in
thun - der - clouds form, And dark is His
scends to the plain, And sweet - ly dis -
firm to the end! Our Mak - er, De -

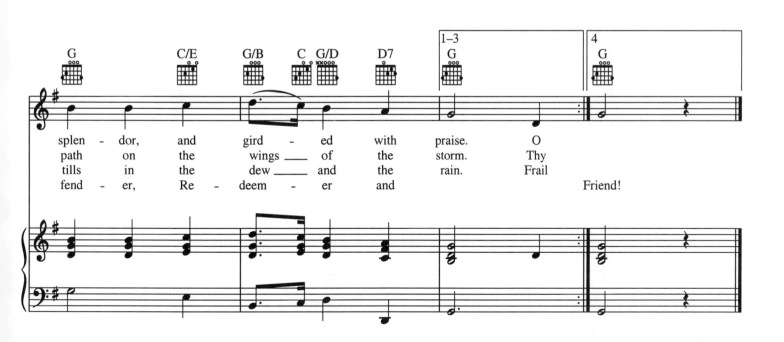

splen - dor, and gird - ed with praise. O
path on the wings ___ of the storm. Thy
tills in the dew ___ and the rain. Frail
fend - er, Re - deem - er and Friend!

THE OLD RUGGED CROSS

By REV. GEORGE BENNARD

Copyright © 1991 by HAL LEONARD CORPORATION
International Copyright Secured   All Rights Reserved

ONWARD, CHRISTIAN SOLDIERS

Words by SABINE BARING-GOULD
Music by ARTHUR S. SULLIVAN

Copyright © 1991 by HAL LEONARD CORPORATION
International Copyright Secured   All Rights Reserved

PRAISE GOD, FROM WHOM ALL BLESSINGS FLOW

Words by THOMAS KEN
Music Attributed to LOUIS BOURGEOIS

Copyright © 1999 by HAL LEONARD CORPORATION
International Copyright Secured   All Rights Reserved

PRAISE TO THE LORD, THE ALMIGHTY

Words by JOACHIM NEANDER
Music from *Erneuerten Gesangbuch*
Harmony by WILLIAM STERNDALE BENNETT

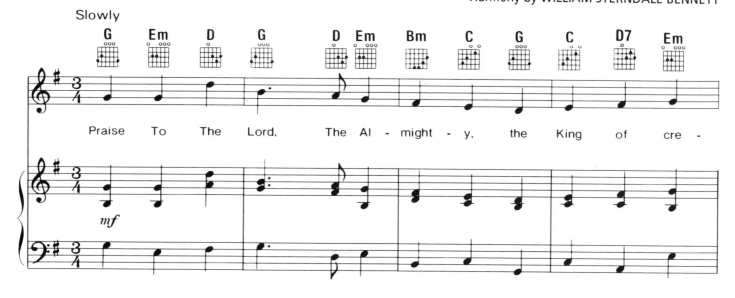

Praise To The Lord, The Al - might - y, the King of cre -

a - tion! O my soul, praise Him, for

He is thy health and sal - va - tion!

Copyright © 1983 by HAL LEONARD CORPORATION
International Copyright Secured All Rights Reserved

ROCK OF AGES

Text by AUGUSTUS M. TOPLADY
Music by THOMAS HASTINGS

Copyright © 1983 by HAL LEONARD CORPORATION
International Copyright Secured   All Rights Reserved

WERE YOU THERE?

African-American Spiritual
Harmony by CHARLES WINFRED DOUGLAS

Were you there when they cru-ci-fied my Lord? (Were you there?) Were you
there when they nailed Him to the tree? (To the tree?) Were you
there when they pierced Him in the side? (In the side?) Were you

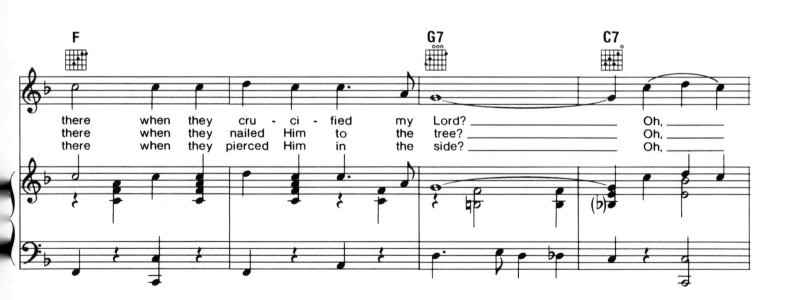

there when they cru-ci-fied my Lord? _____ Oh, _____
there when they nailed Him to the tree? _____ Oh, _____
there when they pierced Him in the side? _____ Oh, _____

Copyright © 1983 by HAL LEONARD CORPORATION
International Copyright Secured   All Rights Reserved

WHAT A FRIEND WE HAVE IN JESUS

Words by JOSEPH SCRIVEN
Music by CHARLES C. CONVERSE

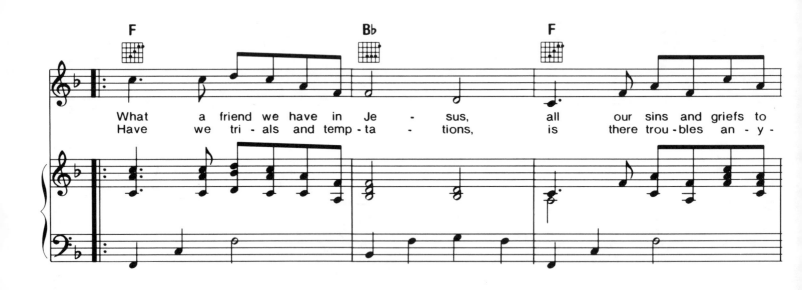

What a friend we have in Je - sus, all our sins and griefs to
Have we tri - als and temp - ta - tions, is there trou - bles an - y -

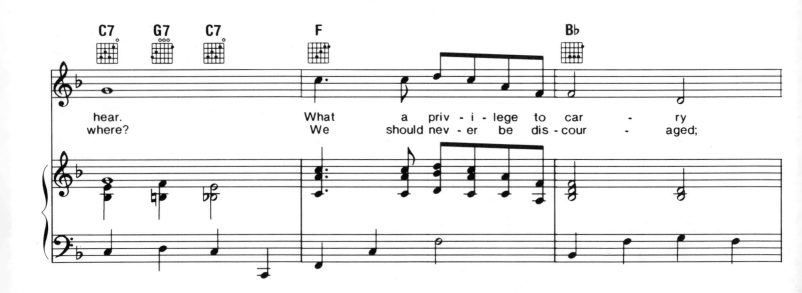

hear. What a priv - i - lege to car - ry
where? We should nev - er be dis - cour - aged;

Copyright © 1983 by HAL LEONARD CORPORATION
International Copyright Secured   All Rights Reserved

3. Are we weak and heavy laden,
cumbered with a load of care?
Precious Savior still our refuge;
take it to the Lord in prayer.
Do thy friends despise, forsake thee?
Take it to the Lord in prayer.
In His arms He'll take and shield thee;
thou will find a solace there.

WHEN I SURVEY THE WONDROUS CROSS

Words by ISAAC WATTS
Music by LOWELL MASON

When I sur-vey the won-drous cross
For-bid it, Lord, that I should

cross   On which the Prince of
boast   Save in the death of

Copyright © 1983 by HAL LEONARD CORPORATION
International Copyright Secured   All Rights Reserved

3. See, from His head, His hands, His feet,
   Sorrow and love flow mingled down
   Did e'er such love and sorrow meet
   Or thorns compose so rich a crown.

4. Were the whole realm of nature mine,
   That were a present far too small.
   Love so amazing so divine,
   Demands my soul, my life, my all.

Exclusive Distributors:

Music Sales Limited

8/9 Frith Street, London W1D 3JB, England.

Music Sales Pty Limited

120 Rothschild Avenue, Rosebery,

NSW 2018, Australia.

Order No. HLE90000638

ISBN 0-7119-8235-X

This book © Copyright 2000 by

Hal Leonard Europe.

Unauthorised reproduction of

any part of this publication by any

means including photocopying is an

infringement of copyright.

Cover by Michael Bell Design.

Photograph (Chichester Cathedral) © Pitkin Unichrome Ltd.

Printed in the USA.

Your Guarantee of Quality:

As publishers, we strive to produce every book to

the highest commercial standards.

The book has been carefully designed to

minimise awkward page turns and to make

playing from it a real pleasure.

Throughout, the printing and binding have

been planned to ensure a sturdy, attractive publication

which should give years of enjoyment.

If your copy fails to meet our high standards, please inform us

and we will gladly replace it.

Music Sales' complete catalogue describes

thousands of titles and is available in full colour sections by

subject, direct from Music Sales Limited.

Please state your areas of interest and send a

cheque/postal order for £1.50 for postage to:

Music Sales Limited, Newmarket Road,

Bury St. Edmunds, Suffolk IP33 3YB, England.

www.musicsales.com